SNEYD PARK

1. Rockleaze extends to the right from Ivywell Road, large houses with round baywindows, facing Durdham Downs. This winter view published by York in 1922.

2. Downleaze joins from Rockleaze facing the downs. This view postally used in 1907.

3. This view is the middle part of Downleaze, which extends in a U shape from Durdham Downs, to join Julian Road. The house on the left "The Old Halt". In earlier times a hostelry known as "The Ostrich". Also named "Durdham Lodge" c.1904.

4. Downleaze, although the caption on this postcard says Stoke Hill, it is infact Downleaze, which extends to opposite the single storey house on the right, and joins Stoke Hill there. The large Houses built in 1899, with fine views of the Downs.

SNEYD PARK

Downleaze.
1130.

5. Downleaze this part extends parallel with the part facing the Downs, again a change in design. This view c.1920's. Today a conservation area protecting the unique architecture of Sneyd Park.

SNEYD PARK

6. Julian Road at the junction with The Avenue, postally used in 1907. This road and the immediate roads around were part of the estate of Stoke House, now Trinity Theological College.

7. Pitch and Pay Lane connects with Julian Road and Church Road. So called because during the 1645 plague, Bristolians came to a style, tossing payments to country folk, at a safe distance, who threw back food. Postcard postally used in 1909.

8. Christ Church was built in 1877, and stood on the corner of Julian Road and Rockleaze Avenue, a United Reform Church the last service held in 1962, and later demolished in favour of Julian Court flats. A garage replaces the houses on the left.

Christ Church, Sneyd Park.

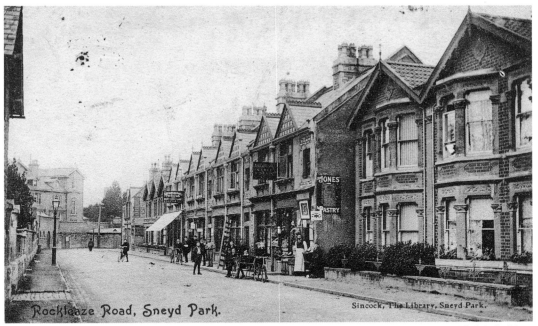

Rockleaze Road, Sneyd Park.

Sincock, The Library, Sneyd Park.

9. Rockleaze Road, this view c.1906, shows a busy row of shops, a window cleaner with his ladder, and a shopkeeper standing outside his shop wearing a large white apron. The houses in the distance the rear view of the houses in Rockleaze.

Rockleaze Avenue, Sneyd Park.

Sincock, The Library, Westbury-on-Trym.

10. Rockleaze Avenue, adjoining with Rockleaze Road, an early view posted in December 1904, and the message reads "Our house is the second on the right".

Old Sneyd Park.

11. Old Sneyd Park showing the house originating from the 17th century. The extensive grounds, which extend from Mariners Way (on the Old Roman Road), to the cliffs above the river Avon. The Estate included a Deer Park, and farm, and two lodges.

Old Sneed Park. No. 1.

12. The imposing front entrance to Old Sneyd Park, (note the different spelling). The owners from the 1870's were Francis Tagart, and several others including the last private owner Sir George White.

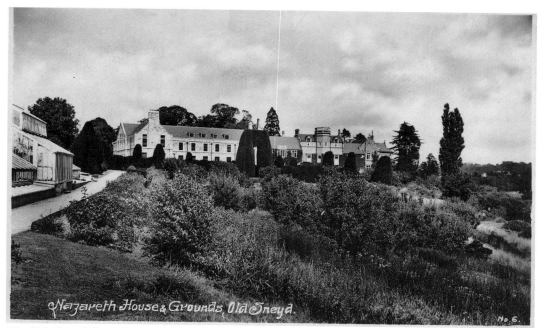

13. Old Sneyd Park House became Nazareth House in the 1950's and changed to a Catholic School School for orphan boys. The school closed and the house demolished in 1972, after a fire. Parts of the wall surrounding the kitchen garden are all that now remains.

14. Cook's Folly from the river Avon, showing the turreted house on the extreme right. Dr. Goodeve built the house onto the original tower in 1857; he lived there until he died in 1884. To the left properties with extensive greenhouse and gardens, making the most of sun on the South site.

Sneyd Park from Sea Walls.

15. Part of Sneyd Park boarders the river Avon, from Sea Walls to Sea Mills; many large houses took advantage of the aspect with its south facing views. This early view c.1905 shows on the extreme right Towerhurst, and just below Sea Walls Villa.

VIEW FROM SEA WALLS. CLIFTON DOWNS, SHOWING COOK'S FOLLY.   B. B. 54. L.

16. The same view from Sea Walls, Sea Walls Villa, on the right, which was built in the 1860's. Pulled down in early 1972's for housing and flats.

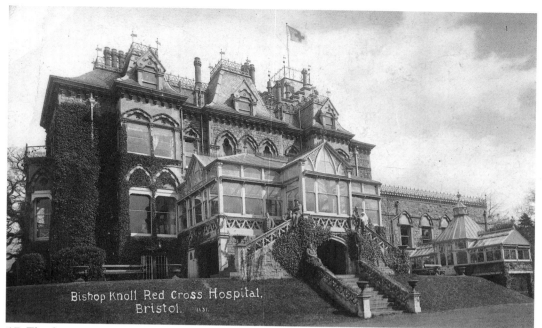

17. The front entrance of Bishop Knoll Red Cross Hospital a private house converted to a hospital during 1914-18 war to receive injured soldiers from the front. Owned by Mr. & Mrs. Bush, Bristolians, who worked in Australia for 35 years. They ran the hospital together.

18. Bishop Knoll Hospital, nurses with wounded soldiers recovering, they encouraged many Australian soldiers as patients. Postally used in 1916, message reads: "Philip able to walk pretty well now".

19. Downleaze Road. Today known as Downleaze, an early view from Stoke Hill end posted in 1905.

20. The Avenue a tree lined road, which extends from Julian Road through to Sea Walls Road. Postally used in 1907.

21. Ivywell Road, the beginning of which faces the Durdham Downs in the direction of Sea Walls, from the corner with Rockleaze. The road in the foreground known today as the Circular Road.

22. Further along Ivywell Road, Well House originally a farmhouse to Old Sneyd Park estate. This view postally used in 1916.

23. Looking down Stoke Hill towards the centre of the village. Beyond the garage, on the left shops newly built. Glen House in the distance and open fields.

24. Stoke Cottages built in 1885. These cottages recognisable today, the fields beyond that later became Druid Hill.

25. Stoke village, near Bristol. This view before Stoke Bishop became part of Bristol in 1904. Children standing in the snow near the large tree by the Diamond Jubilee fountain. The signpost directs to the left Sea Mills Station.

26. A 1930's view from Tagart's fountain looking towards the shops in Stoke Hill, on the corner of Old Sneed Avenue. Looking through one of the windows of the fountain, a shop nearing completion.

27. The fountain commemorating Queen Victoria's Diamond Jubilee in 1897, was donated by Francis Tagart, who lived at Old Sneed Park House. The cottage on the left, the old Post Office. The postcard postally used in 1903.

28. Stoke Bishop school was built on land purchased from Mr. Budgett of Stoke House in 1874. The school was damaged by bombs in 1940, and a new School was built at Cedar Park in 1951, the building delayed because of the war, 1939-45.

29. The panoramic view of the centre of Stoke Bishop c.1934, from Butchers Hill, now Druid Hill. The Diamond Jubilee fountain can be seen. The ivy covered house on the right, Glen House, and beyond, the houses in Old Sneed Avenue.

30. Another interesting view of the village, taken further up Druid Hill. The house to the left of the fountain demolished c.1979, for road realignment. The spire of St. Mary's Church in the distance.

31. Hollybush Lane, which extends from the top of Druid Hill and bordering Stoke Bishop, it reaches Saville Road on Durdham Downs. Very much still a lane, trees and shrubs have obscured views. But at the top St. Mary's Church's spire can be seen.

Ye Olde - Stoke Abbey Farm.   Date 1670.
For fine milk, cream, clotted cream & all dairy produce delivered to City - Clifton & Suburbs twice daily.

32. Stoke Abbey Farm in Parry's Lane dates from 1670. Their deliveries of milk and all dairies produce to the City and Clifton twice daily. The old farm surrounded by the houses of Stoke Bishop, and is a busy milk delivery depot today.

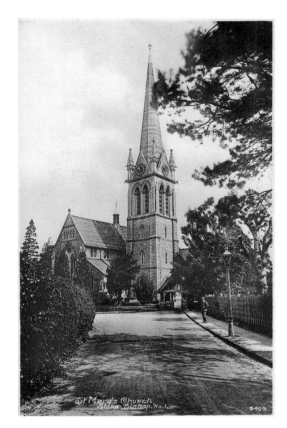

33. St. Mary Magdalene church, the parish church of Stoke Bishop, was built in 1860. In 1871 the nave was extended, and the west porch, the tower and the spire were added. The first vicar was David Wright 1860-95. The Lych Gate was built as a memorial to local men killed in the 1914-18 war.

34. The Memorial Cross stands at the junction of Stoke Hill and Downleaze. It was unveiled on May 20th 1920 a memorial to men killed in the 1914-18 war

35. Druid Stoke Farm c.1910. The farm cottage with all the family posing for the picture. Notice the latticed summerhouse on the right.

36. Druid Road a late 1930's view, new fencing and young trees planted. The road joins with Stoke Hill and through to Mariners Drive.

37. Old Sneed Road joins the village in Stoke Hill and at the far end with Old Sneed Avenue. This early 1930's view shows the parish church of St. Mary's spire, above the trees.

38. Kewstoke Road begins in Stoke Hill, just beyond Stoke Bishop Village Hall. The road c.1930's, with detached and semi-detached houses, extend across Hollybush Lane through to Parry's Lane.

39. Old Sneed Avenue which starts in Druid Hill, by the shops, and bends round by Avon Way, to join with Old Sneed Road further up in Stoke Hill.

40. Old Sneed Road a different angle of the road from picture 37. Large detached houses typical of houses built in the area during the 1930's

41. The shops built in Druid Hill c.1938, and continuing up the hill flat roofed houses, joining further around the corner at the top of the hill with Shirehampton Road and Parry's Lane. The small house on the right demolished 1979.

42. The newsagent and post office on the corner of Old Sneed Avenue at the bottom of Stoke Hill. The shops centre in Druid Hill, still quite rural beyond.

COOMBE DINGLE

43. The Dingle c.1915, from Canford Lane. The charming cottages survive today as one cottage. The road follows the river Trym, joins Westbury Lane near the junction with Sylvan Way.

44. The wide approach from The Dingle, as it enters New Road, now Canford Lane. This view in the early 1930's shows three detached houses 330, 332 and 334 Canford Lane.

COOMBE DINGLE

45. Ethel (Nee Griffin) Watkins and friends sitting in a car outside of 3 Dingle Road. The Wesleyan Methodist Church in the background. The first services held there in 1897. The land for building was given by the Grandfather of Mr D. A. Watkins, and Mr J. V. Watkins.

46. A man and small girl, on a small bridge over the river Trym, a delightful view c.1910.

47. Dolly (nee Griffin) Hutton, her sister Ethel (nee Griffin) and their Mother outside No. 3 Dingle Road in 1921.

48. The Dingle descends to river level by this cottage. The two ladies and their children, (the same as in picture 43). At this point there is a bridge across the river Trym.

49. A view looking down onto the cottage c.1915. A well attended garden, and the river Trym flowing past, the bridge mentioned in picture 48, can be seen on the right. The cottage liable to flooding was pulled down c.1942.

COOMBE DINGLE

View at Combe Dingle.

50. The Dingle, a postally used postcard in 1905. This view outside of Apple Tree Cottage, (the steps are still there today), is on the corner of Grove Road.

Rose Cottage Tea Gardens. Combe Dingle.

51. On the opposite corner with Grove Road in The Dingle, Rose Cottage Tea Gardens. One of the many tea gardens popular in the early years of the last century.

The Apple Tree, Coombe Dingle. No. 1183.

52. Apple Tree Cottage, the railings can be recognised from picture 50. A charming cottage covered with ivy and wisteria. Postcard postally used in 1906.

Apple tree Tea Gardens, Coombe Dingle, Nr. Bristol. No. 1493.

53. The garden behind Apple Tree Cottage, another popular tea garden. This time swings for the children. This postcard c.1906.

54. Grove Side Tea Gardens, tables laid up with table cloths, and flowers in the centre of the tables, awaiting customers.

55. A view of the cottage in Grove Side Tea Gardens. A delightful view of the family, and customers. The proprietor Mr. W. Lee. The donkey used to haul water from a pump in the Dingle.

COOMBE DINGLE

Clack Cottage, nr. Clack Old Mill.

56. Coombe Dingle, Clack Mill cottages, adjoining the old Mill. The family sitting in their garden. The sign on the porch, "Hansford and Co. Mineral Waters". Probably the drink on sale there.

Clack Mills, Coombe Dingle. Nº 1436.

57. Clack Mill c.1909. In use until 1937, situated between Shirehampton and Dingle Road.

COOMBE DINGLE

58. Coombe House, a large house with extensive grounds, overlooks the Vale of Coombe Dingle. The entrance from the lodge in Canford Lane. The house is now a home for senior citizens. Postcard postally used in 1916.

59. The Mill in Coombe Dingle, worked by Mr. E. Ball and his sons, who were flour millers c.1916.

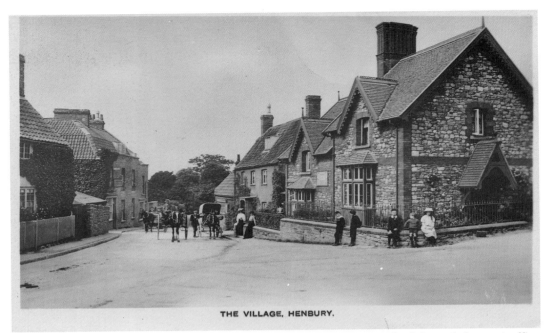

THE VILLAGE, HENBURY.

60. Henbury Village looking down to Henbury Road. Blaise Inn on the left, and the post office the second house on the right. This view c.1910. The children sitting on the low wall by the turning for Church Lane.

Henbury.

61. Looking in the opposite direction, towards Kings Weston Road. This view c.1923. The shop is a bank, London County Westminster and Paris Bank Ltd.

62. The Salutation with early frontage onto the road. This view c.1910 shows a rather shallow ford, with cart tracks. A small boy by piles of stones near the turning to Crow Lane.

63. This view from the ford very deep from heavy rain shows the Salutation Inn with its unchanged frontage, c.1930's. The ford is part of the stream, Hazel Brook (or the Hen) which flows through Blaise Caste Estate.

64. In the opposite direction from picture 62-63 showing the ford, a rural scene with a herd of cows. The frontages of the Salutation Inn just in view on the left. Published by Viners of Bath.

65. This view from the road adjoining the ford, looking towards the first houses in Henbury Road. This card published by Tucks.

66. The cobbled road leading to St. Mary's parish church, Close House and Sexton's Cottage on the right. The church dating from the Norman times. The nave and pillars dating from the 12th century. The parish includes Henbury, Brentry and Hallen.

67. Within the grounds of Blaise Castle, the walled garden with a pathway, and a decorative Grecian urn and neat flowerbeds, and the tower of St. Mary's Church.

The Manor House, Henbury.

Sincock, The Library, Westbury-on-Trym.

68. The Manor House built by John Sampson before 1677. Built of Cotswold stone, with gables and a square porch. The last private owner Major Sampson-Way, who inherited the house in 1927 who died in 1947.

HENBURY COURT HOTEL. 88.

York Series.

69. Henbury Court was built by Thomas Stock in 1807, and took up residency in 1812. He was a sugar refiner by trade, and lived there until his death in 1833. A great family man. He had associations with John Wesley, and became a Methodist.

70. Westmoreland Farm situated at the village end of Crow Lane. The Salutation Inn and church tower can be seen between the farm buildings. named after the Countess of Westmorland, who granted the land to Sir Thomas Fane in 1639.

71. The Elms in Henbury Hill, built of Cotswold Stone in the 17th century. The farm owned by Mr. W. Biggs a dairyman. The postcard posted in 1908, from Worthy Farm, Henbury, with an order for dairy produce.

72. Aust farm a 17th century farmhouse, not in Henbury as the postcard describes, but in Knovill Close, Lawrence Weston and is surrounded by houses built in the 1950's. This view of the farmer and his family c.1910.

73. The Thatched Lodge in Kings Weston Lane, contemporary with John Nash, and his design of the diary and orangery in the 19th century. A bomb in the last war destroyed it, and the site used to build toilets.

HENBURY

BLAISE CASTLE, HENBURY.

74. Blaise Castle built on a high plateau, is an 18th century folly, built by Thomas Farr a Bristol merchant in 1766. The name derived from a medieval chapel, St. Blasius, near the site of an old Roman Fort.

Blaise Castle House 877. Bristol

75. Blaise Castle House built in 1796 for John Harford, a well-known Quaker banker. The house designed by William Paty. This view in 1938 shows fencing and gates to the house, and the balustrade intact. These were damaged during Military occupation during the last war.

76. John Nash designed the Diary in the early 19th century, with a charming thatched roof, and it is very cool inside, even on the warmest day.

77. The Orangery (now Conservatory), to the house built from a design by John Nash, who also designed the dairy, they were completed c.1806.

THE UPPER GATE, BLAISE CASTLE WOODS.

78. This is a view of the Upper Lodge in Henbury Hill, a design by Humphery Repton a landscape gardener, and creator of the driveway to Blaise Castle House, and other gateways, pathways, roads, viewing areas and cottages, enhancing Blaise Castle Estate.

Blaize Castle Lodge, & Henbury Hill. 1193

79. A view of the Upper Lodge entrance from Henbury Hill. Behind the·man in the road, the hill descending towards Henbury village. Published by Viner and posted in 1916.

80. The Inner Lodge a short distance from picture 79 on the driveway to Blaise Castle House. Built predminatly of wood, with a small porch and thatched roof.

81. Further along the same drive through the woods towards Blaise House, the Head Forester's Lodge. A little girl by the rhododendrons. A delightful view. Postally used in 1931.

82. Stratford Mill brought from Chew Valley in Somerset, when Chew Valley reservoir was being constructed. The mill adjoining Hazel Brook (or Hen) dates from 1796.

83. This road enters the grounds of Blaise Castle Estate at Coombe Dingle. This view by the Beech Wood. Further along it joins the road from the Upper lodge, by a bridge over the Hazel Brook, then continues to Blaise Castle House.

84. Echo Gate from the Coombe Dingle end, and it lives up to its description!. Among the many walks from this gate, Blaise Castle folly can be reached up a fairly steep path.

85. Arbutus Grove another delightful path off of the main pathway, from The Dingle, in Coombe Dingle.

86. Blaise Hamlet built for retired workers of Blaise estate, and designed by John Nash in 1810. It lies on the Hallen Road, and the houses built around a miniature green, a sundial in the middle. Picture by Garratt, postally used in 1943.

BLAISE HAMLET, HENBURY. No. 575.

87. An earlier view of the hamlet, showing two of the cottage, one thatched and the other tiled. All the front doors were designed in different positions to maintain a degree of privacy. Postal used in 1918.

INDEX